Why Do We Pray?

Miranda Nerland
Illustrated by Hayley O'Neal

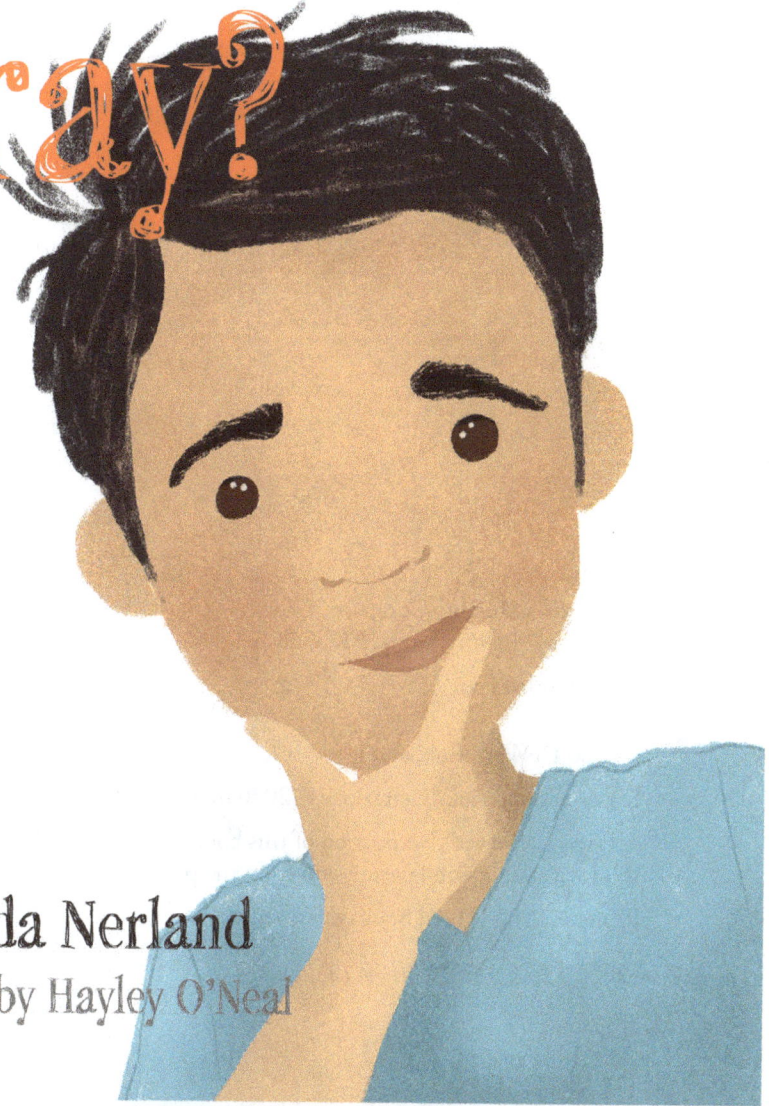

Why Do We Pray?
DeWard Publishing Company, LLC.
P.O. Box 290696, Tampa, FL 33687

www.deward.com

© 2020 DeWard Publishing

Cover and interior illustrations © 2020 by Hayley O'Neal

Printed in the United States of America.

ISBN: 978-1-947929-10-4

For Marit,
who taught us to pray.

Have you ever wanted to talk to God?
To whisper your secret wish right into His ear,
or ask God a very important question?

Have you ever wanted to shout
out a great big "Thank YOU!" to God for everything
you have or ask Him to help you make the right choice?

You can! Every time you whisper, ask, or shout out to God,
you are saying a prayer that God will hear.

(1 John 5:14)

When you pray, imagine this: you are talking to the very
same God who made the whole world.

He's the same God who parted the Red Sea for Moses,
who helped David defeat Goliath, and who brought down the walls of
Jericho for His special people Israel. He's the King of Kings
and the Lord of Lords, and He wants to hear from you.

God hears your prayers no matter where you are.

Elijah shouted on a mountaintop and God heard him.

Hannah whispered in the temple and God heard her.

God heard Paul's prayer in prison, Daniel's prayers when he was far from home, and Jonah's prayer from the belly of a great fish deep under the sea.

God even heard Jesus' prayers on the cross.

(1 Samuel 2, Jonah 2, Daniel 6, 1 Kings 18, Matthew 27)

Jesus was God's son and He prayed too.
When Jesus was on Earth, he talked to God all the time,
and lots of His prayers are written down in the Bible for us to read.
Jesus even prayed one very special prayer to teach his friends
how to pray—a prayer filled with every single thing that God
wants to hear from the people He loves so much.

(Luke 11:1-4)

Jesus' perfect prayer reminds us
to be respectful when we talk to our
Heavenly Father.

We are so blessed that the holy God who
lives in Heaven wants us to call Him Father,
just like Jesus did!

(Matthew 6:9, Psalm 103:13)

Jesus' perfect prayer also reminds us that
God wants us to ask Him for help.

When you ask God for the things you need, you show Him that
you trust Him to take care of you and that you believe all
the promises He has made will come true.

(Matthew 6:11, Psalm 23)

DEAR GOD, THANK YOU FOR MOM GOD
DAD AND MY FRIENDS.
PLEASE TAKE CARE OF
US AND HELP ABIGAIL
TO FEEL BETTER SOON.
THANK YOU FOR JESUS AND
I LIKED THE SUNSHINE YESTERDAY.
WE LOVE YOU GOD
JESUS NAME AMEN

You can also ask God to protect you.
When it's hard to be kind, hard to share, hard to forgive,
or hard to tell the truth, tell God about it.

Ask Him to help you do the right thing
all the time, even when it's hard.

(Matthew 6:13, Psalm 16:1)

You can even talk to God when you've done
something wrong. When it's hard to be kind,
hard to share, or hard to tell the truth,
God wants to hear about it.

That's called confessing.

Even though God sees everything and already knows all
about it, God wants you to share these things with Him.

He promises to forgive you and also promises to be with you,
so you can make a better choice next time.

(Matthew 6:12, Psalm 32)

But remember: Jesus' perfect prayer also reminds us
that we need to seek God's will when we pray.
That means that we always respect God's answer,
even when it's different from the answer that we want.

HOW goD ANSweReD
mY PRAYer:

☐ YES

☐ No

☒ waiT

When we ask for things in prayer, God sometimes says yes,
and He sometimes says no. He sometimes even asks us to wait
a little while. No matter the answer, you can count on
God to hear you every time you ask for help.

(Matthew 6:10, Psalm 27:14)

Of course, there is so much more
to prayer than asking.

Sometimes when you pray, you can
just tell God about how great He is.

That's called praise.

(Psalm 9:1)

Try it sometime. Talk to God and don't ask for anything. Just tell Him thank you for every good thing you have, or spend some time thanking Him for the amazing world He made for you and me.

(1 Thessalonians 5:18, Psalm 107:8-9)

Sometimes our prayers are all about someone else.
God wants us to pray for one another. He wants us to pray
for the people we know who are sad or hurting or sick.

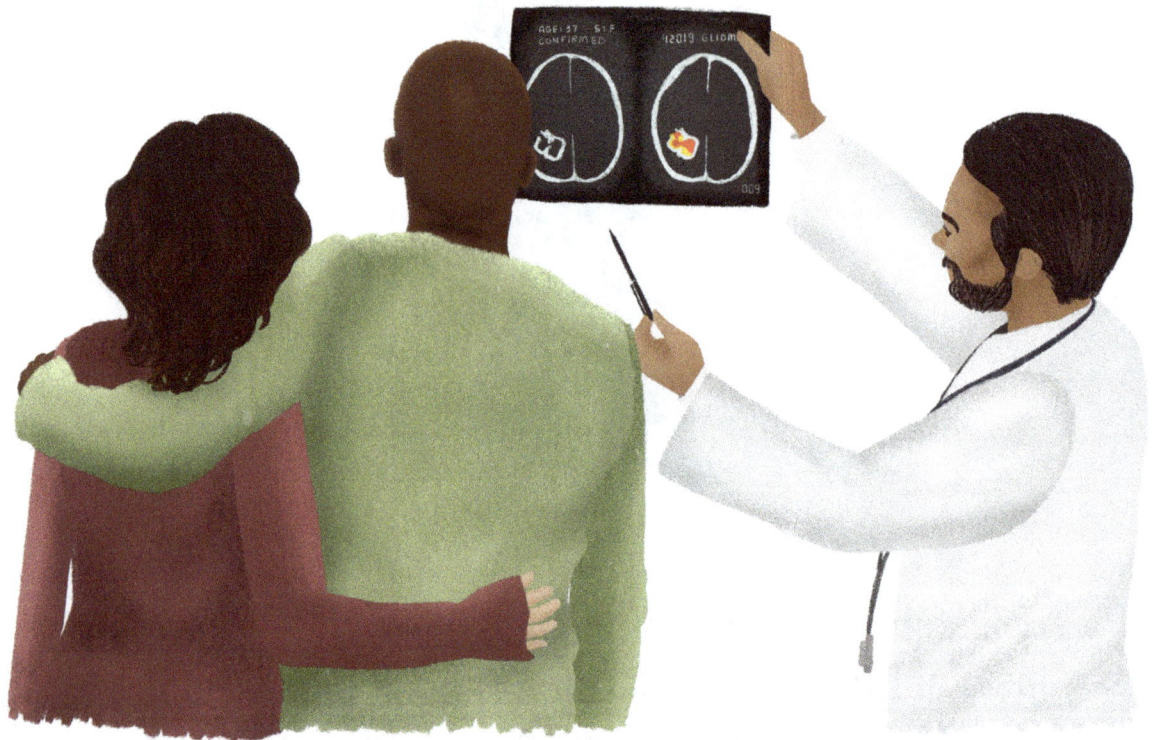

He wants us to pray for people who need help, or who
do not have everything they need. No matter how small you are,
you are a great big helper when you pray for someone else.

(Ephesians 6:18)

Here's the best part,
God wants to hear from you.
Your thoughts and feelings
are important to Him,
and He wants you to talk
to him every single day.

(1 Thessalonians 5:17)

God wants you to pray to Him because He loves
to hear from his people, but He also knows that prayer
is good for you. Praying to our Creator reminds us that He
is in charge of everything. This keeps us from worrying,
reminds us to be grateful, and gives us a special kind of
peace deep in our hearts.

(Philippians 4:6-7)

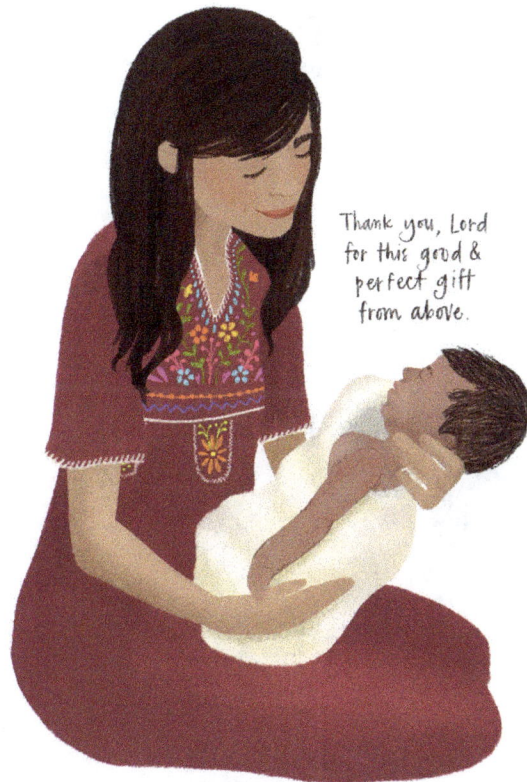

Thank you, Lord
for this good &
perfect gift
from above.

Even though we can pray anywhere and anytime,

prayer is a big part of what we do in worship together.

(James 5:16)

When you set down your books and pencils and close your eyes, you are showing God and others that you are paying close attention to the words of the prayer.

You are showing God and others that nothing is more important to you right now than praying.

When you bow your head,
you are showing God that you respect him,
and that you believe He is the biggest
and the strongest and the smartest.

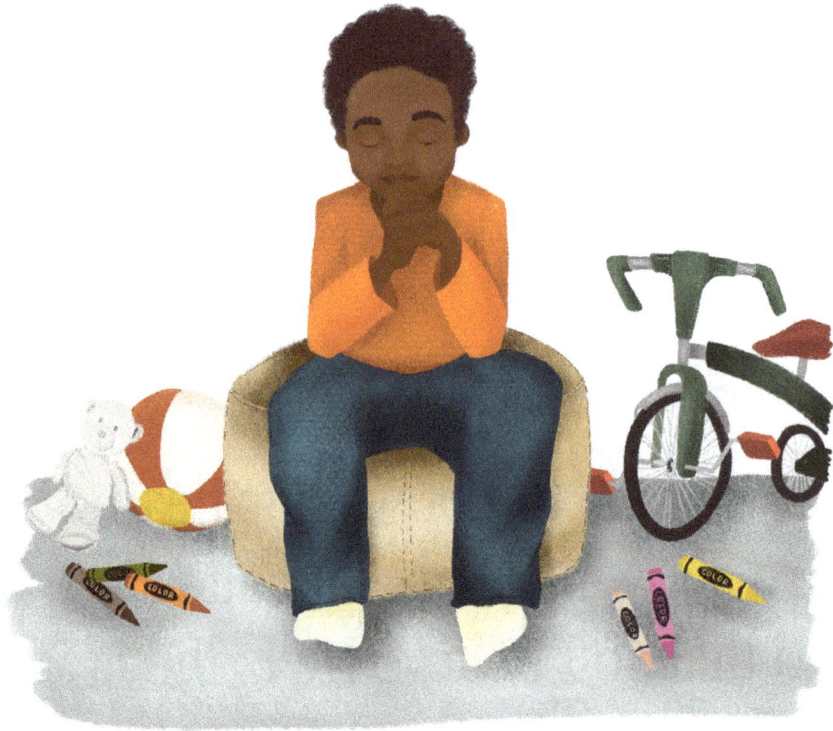

The Bible promises us that great things can happen
if we pray to God with faith and confidence.

We are so blessed that Jesus took the time to show us
how to pray, and we are blessed that God wants to hear what
we think and feel every day. Our prayers are beautiful to God
and are one more way we can honor Him and show
God how much we love Him.

(Psalm 141:2)

More Why? books by Miranda Nerland:

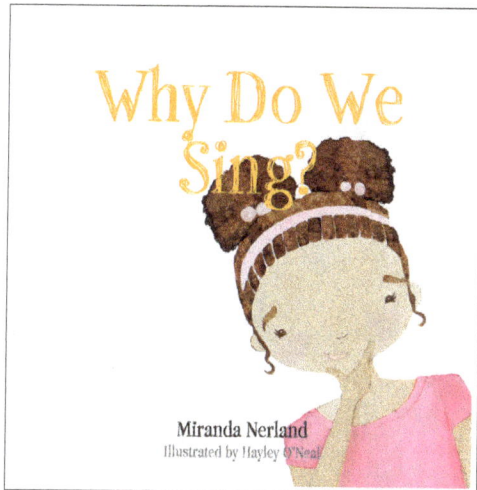

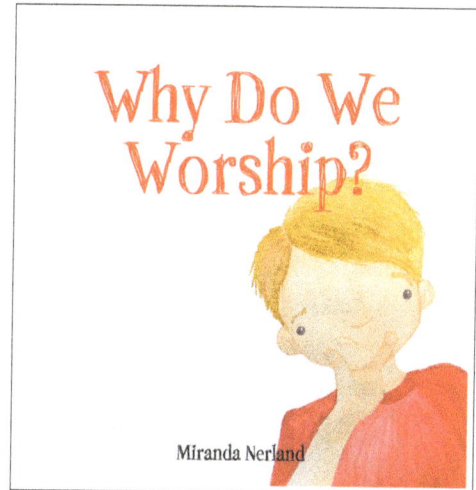

DeWard™ kids

www.deward.com